WORTH FIGHTING FOR

The aim of Zenith Books is to present the history of minority groups in the United States and their participation in the growth and development of the country. Through histories and biographies written by leading historians in collaboration with established writers for young people, Zenith Books will increase the awareness of minority groups members of their own heritage and at the same time develop among all people an understanding and appreciation of that heritage.

SHELLEY UMANS is a specialist in reading instruction and is a member of the instructional staff of Teachers College, Columbia University. For more than ten years, she has been a consultant to many major urban school systems throughout the United States. She is the author of *New Trends in Reading Instruction* and *Designs for Reading Programs*.

DR. JOHN HOPE FRANKLIN, currently Professor of History at the University of Chicago, has also taught at Brooklyn College, Fisk University, and Howard University. For the year 1962–1963, he was William Pitt Professor of American History and Institutions at Cambridge University in England. He is the author of many books including *From Slavery to Freedom, The Militant South, Reconstruction After the Civil War,* and *The Emancipation Proclamation*.

AGNES McCARTHY is an Editor in the Department of School Services and Publications at Wesleyan University. She has had teaching experience in both the elementary grades and junior high school. Among Miss McCarthy's other books are *Let's Go to Vote, Let's Go to a Court,* and *New York State; Its Land and People*.

DR. LAWRENCE REDDICK is Professor of History and Politics at Coppin State Teachers College in Baltimore, Maryland. He formerly taught at Dillard University, Atlanta University, Alabama State College, and the City College of New York. Dr. Reddick was for a number of years Curator of the Schomburg Collection of the New York Public Library. His most recent book is *Crusader Without Violence: A Biography of Martin Luther King, Jr.*

COLLEEN BROWNING teaches art at the City College of New York. She has won art awards from the Carnegie Institute, the National Academy of Design, and the National Institute of Arts and Letters. She has illustrated many books for young people in such series as Best-in-Children's Books and Junior Deluxe Edition Classics.

WORTH
FIGHTING FOR

A HISTORY OF THE NEGRO IN THE UNITED STATES
DURING THE CIVIL WAR AND RECONSTRUCTION

Agnes McCarthy and
Lawrence Reddick, Ph.D.

Illustrated by Colleen Browning

ZENITH BOOKS

DOUBLEDAY & COMPANY, INC., GARDEN CITY, NEW YORK

1965

The Zenith Books edition, published simultaneously in hard-bound and paperback volumes, is the first publication of *Worth Fighting For*.

Zenith Books edition: 1965

CONTENTS

9729

PART I

PREPARING FOR FREEDOM

CHAPTER 1

The Soldier That Nobody Wanted

The land was quiet. Dawn had not yet come. Inside Fort Sumter, Union soldiers waited tensely. Fort Sumter, in Charleston, South Carolina, belonged to the United States Government. Southerners had threatened to attack the fort. They probably meant it. President Abraham Lincoln thought so, at least. He was sending a ship with supplies to Fort Sumter. The soldiers hoped the supplies would come before the attack.

But it was too late for hopes. For on April 12, 1861, the still morning air was broken with the sound of cannon fire. The Southern Army closed in. Men began to fall and die. On April 14, Major Robert Anderson of the United States Army had to surrender the fort to the Confederate forces. This was the beginning of the Civil War. Few men believed it then, but this war was to last for four terrible years. Courage was going to be tested. Blood was going to be spilt. And, at the end, freedom was going to raise her golden lamp. Its light was going to fall on the Negro slaves.

From the very beginning, the Negro believed that the war was a war for freedom. Four million slaves in the South felt, "Thank God! At last it's come." This was to be the war that struck off their chains and set them free. In the North, Negroes who were already free wanted to serve the cause of liberty. The day after Fort Sumter was taken, President Lincoln called for 75,000 men to fight in the Union Army. Negroes were among the first to volunteer. But they were turned away! "No Negro soldiers are wanted" was the answer they got.

In New York City, some free Negroes formed a club and held drilling and target practice. They

wanted to fight and to be good fighters at that. But the police broke up their drills and practices. "No Negroes are going to be soldiers," they were told.

In Philadelphia, Detroit, and Chicago, free Negroes offered to perform another kind of help. "We will go into the South," they said, "and band the slaves together. We will make armies of them, and fight the Confederate soldiers from inside the South." The idea was turned down. "We don't need Negro armies," the answer came again.

"What's wrong?" the Negro asked himself. "Can't white men see that this is our war as much as it is theirs? Don't they understand that we want to carry that same freedom to our brothers in the South? Why are we not allowed to fight?" Frederick Douglass, who had escaped from slavery many years before, said, "The Union fights with its soft white hand, while it keeps its black iron hand chained helpless behind it." In his newspaper, the *Douglass Monthly*, he begged the Union Army to arm the Negro. "Just the sight of Negro troops on the banks of the Mississippi would send the Confederates running," Douglass said.

But this kind of argument did little good. In the first years of the war, white Northerners didn't see the war in the light that the Negro saw it. For the Negro, the war was to set black men free. For most white Northerners, the war was a fight to save the Union. The southern states had broken away from this Union. They had set up their own government. Now they must be brought back into the Union by force. That was the way the Northerners saw it. It was a "white man's war." Besides, there was much prejudice against the Negro, even in the North. White soldiers didn't want to fight with Negroes by their side. Some white men felt that the Negro had little courage, and would run away when the fighting became hard and the battle bloody.

Not everybody felt this way. Long before the war, many whites had worked side by side with the Negro in his struggle for freedom. And now, with the war begun, they worked with him in his struggle for a place in the Union Army. Horace Greeley, a New York newspaper publisher, wrote a letter to Lincoln. Greeley asked the President to make the war a moral issue, that is, to make the war a battle for human rights and to let the Negro join the battle. Lincoln replied to Greeley by saying, "My paramount object in this struggle is to save the Union, and is not either to save or destroy slavery. If I could save the Union without freeing any slave I would do it, and if I could save the Union by freeing some and leaving others alone I would also do that. . . ."

A Union general, George B. McClellan, went even further. No matter how the war turned out, he said, slaves would still be slaves at the end, and masters would be masters. When another Union general, John C. Frémont, freed the slaves in Missouri, President Lincoln had the order of freedom canceled. In some cases the Union Army actually helped slave-owners to keep their slaves.

Still the Negroes kept their belief that this was a Freedom War. And, strangely enough, they kept on believing in Lincoln, in spite of what he had written in his letter to Greeley. Perhaps they remembered what Lincoln had said some thirty years before, when he was still a young man—that he would like to destroy "that *thing*" (the *thing* being slavery). Lincoln moved slowly. Many Negroes called him "the slow coach at Washington." But they believed he was moving toward their view of freedom.

Preparing for Freedom

Before the war, Lincoln had spoken out against slavery. Now that he was a wartime President, he had to speak with caution. He wanted the Union to win this war, and to do that, he could not say all that might have been in his heart. One big problem for him was the border states—Delaware, Maryland, Kentucky, and Missouri. These were states where slavery existed, but they had remained loyal to the Union and were fighting on the Union side. If Lincoln had said that the war was to do away with slavery, these states might have gone over to the Confederate side. And, in the early stages of the war, this might have been a death-blow to the Union, for already the South was winning battles right and left.

If only Lincoln had known early in the war what a powerful fighting force the Negroes could be. Deep in their hearts, they knew more than most white men did. They knew that the war could bring the glory of freedom to men who had been slaves all their lives. They knew that their country would be stronger when it was all free, not just half-free. Believing these things, they could bring faith and courage to the battle. Men fight hard when freedom is at stake. But now, turned away from the army, told that they were not wanted, all they could do was wait and pray for a time to prove themselves. For the Negro was used to fighting for freedom. He had been doing it for hundreds of years.

CHAPTER 2

The Fight Begins

The first Negro slaves were brought from Africa. They were forced aboard the ships in chains; they traveled in chains; and they landed on the soil of America and were sold, still in chains. The white men in charge knew that their black "cargo" wanted to be free. Slave ships were heavily armed so that the crew could crush any possible uprising.

In spite of chains and guns, however, some Negroes managed to strike a blow for freedom before they even reached these shores. Some committed suicide, and found their freedom in death. On a few ships, Negroes managed to carry out a mutiny, that is to take over the ship by overpowering the crew. One successful mutiny took place in 1839 on a ship called the *Amistad*. The slaves killed the crew. Later the mutineers were picked up off the coast of Long Island. The United States Supreme Court ruled that the mutineers were free men.

But most Negro slaves were not so lucky. The days that lay ahead would be sad ones. They had been brought to this country to be sold to farmers

On large plantations, the slaves worked long hours doing such things as picking cotton.

and plantation-owners. They were used to working the land in Africa. They were needed in America to grow tobacco, rice, sugar cane, and, most important of all, cotton. The slave was thought of as a valuable bit of farm equipment, not as a man.

On large plantations, the work day was sometimes eighteen to twenty hours long. There was no pay, of course. "Home" for most slaves was a small, cold hut, with the earthen floor for a bed. "Dinner" was most often some sort of mush or coarse food. The boys and girls who were too young to work had no shoes, and only a sort of long shirt with which to cover themselves. They were fed their meals out of a large, common bowl, just as if they were so many little pigs.

On small farms, the owner usually worked side by side with his slaves in the field. This sometimes led to better treatment. On large plantations, the master was frequently away from home. The field hands worked under the eye of the overseer. The overseer was hired by the owner of the plantation, and his job was to get the plantation to produce big crops. To do this, the overseer worked the slaves without mercy. He used the whip to get the last drop of labor out of them. He used the whip as a punishment for slowing up. And sometimes he used the whip just to show who was "boss."

As for the masters, some were kind. But many were as bad as the overseers. The law did not protect the slave. Masters could quite easily get away with the murder of a slave. Hundreds of slaves were actually beaten to death.

The slaves' lives were filled with hardship. Each day might bring some new cruelty. Worst of all, they had no freedom. A few slaves accepted this kind of life. But most went on fighting for freedom in the best way they could. On the plantations just as on the slave ships, there were cases of suicide. In 1807 some slaves who had just arrived in Charleston starved themselves to death. Now and then, a slave would purposely cut off his hand or foot so that he could not be sold and sent away from his wife and children.

In many cases, slaves rose up against the master and gave back blow for blow. Sometimes they killed their masters by poisoning their food. Such acts were usually done by one or two Negroes, working alone, who could not bear that life of slavery any longer. In most cases, those caught were put to death.

From time to time before the Civil War, Negroes had banded together to revolt against their white masters. The whites were always on guard against this. They hired men to keep watch and sent spies to listen for any such plans of rebellion. So, many of these plans never saw the light of day. Those involved were caught and punished, and that was that. But some of the revolts got quite far along before they were stopped.

When the masters heard that a revolt had been planned, the slaves who were involved were caught and punished.

One such revolt was planned and led by Gabriel Prosser in Henrico County, Virginia. The planning had taken many months and over a thousand slaves were to take part. Weapons, such as clubs and swords, were gathered. The day was set for August 30, 1800. That afternoon, outside of Richmond, the slaves gathered to march on the city. But a great storm came and the going was hard. In addition, two house slaves had informed the whites about the revolt. The Governor of Virginia called for soldiers. They came and captured the Negroes. Prosser and some others ran away, but he was recaptured. When questioned he refused to confess. He was put to death with thirty-five others. One of the captured men said:

"I have nothing more to offer than what George Washington would have had to offer. . . . I have ventured my life in endeavoring to obtain the liberty of my countrymen, and am a willing sacrifice to their cause."

Such words struck fear into the hearts of the whites. All around them they felt this wish for freedom, this great wish that led enslaved men to risk their lives. The whites took even more care than before to destroy revolts before they ever got started, but still Negroes were willing to take the risk.

One such Negro was Denmark Vesey. He was a free man who lived in Charleston, South Carolina.

He worked as a carpenter. Though a slave no longer, he never stopped wanting all slaves to be free. He planned a revolt, chose men to help him, and began to get weapons together. Perhaps as many as nine thousand Negroes and their white friends were involved. The date was set for the second Sunday in July 1822, but somehow the word got out. So Vesey pushed the date ahead a month. Everyone did not get word of this new date. The masters had gotten wind of what was being planned. They moved in and arrested many of the Negroes. Forty-seven were put to death. Four whites who had helped were put in prison.

After the Vesey revolt, white Southerners became filled with even more fear. The 1820s were years of panic. More laws were passed to control and punish those who planned and led revolts. White men who helped the Negroes in these plans were also hung.

Was this to be the end of revolts? No. One of the bloodiest took place on August 21, 1831. This was the day that Nat Turner, a slave from Southampton County, Virginia, struck his blow against slavery. He began by killing his master and his master's family. Other Negroes in the revolt killed their masters, until, within twenty-four hours, sixty whites had been killed. State and federal troops moved in and overpowered the Negroes. Turner was executed.

Fear led to cruelty and murder. Bloodshed led to

John Brown was hanged on December 2, 1859, for leading a revolt at Harper's Ferry, Virginia, in October 1859. This revolt is known as "John Brown's Raid."

bloodshed. The South was seldom a place of happy slaves singing and dancing around the cabins, or of kindly masters handing out presents. When such things happened, they were most unusual. Slavery made the whole South a place of violence. Sometimes the violence did not come to the surface, but it was always there. The wish for freedom kept it there.

White men took part in some of the Negro revolts. In October 1859, just before the Civil War, a white man named John Brown led a revolt at Harper's Ferry, Virginia (now a part of West Virginia). His aim was to capture the United States arsenal there and get arms to fight the Virginia slaveholders. To help him, he had fourteen white men and five Negroes—not a very big army. Frederick Douglass had sat in on the planning of this rebellion, and had advised against it. Douglass was eager to see Negro freedom. He did not believe in taking over United States Government property, and he did not believe Brown's plan would succeed.

Brown's followers went with him without questions. The old man had a way about him. He had planned this move for years. He had deprived his own family of things so that he might equip this little army. With his men, he did manage to invade the town of Harper's Ferry, hold the arsenal for thirty hours, free some slaves, arm some men, and kill three others.

The United States troops, under the command of Colonel Robert E. Lee, wounded or captured nearly all of Brown's men. Brown was hanged on December 2, 1859. By that time, he had already influenced the entire country by his action, and by his words:

"I pity the poor in bondage that have none to help them. . . . You may dispose of me easily, but this question is still to be settled—the Negro question—the end of that is not yet."

CHAPTER 3

The Underground Railroad

Many slave-owners carried a gun all day and slept with it beneath the pillow at night. They were afraid that a slave might rush into the room and strike them down.

While most revolts were put down fairly quickly, the slaves had another way of winning freedom. That was by running away, running north to freedom. And slave-owners sometimes found it difficult or impossible to catch the slave and bring him back.

Sometimes a slave might plan his escape all alone. If he were fairly light-skinned, he might disguise himself a bit more as a white man and travel north that way. Or he might write a note, saying that he was making a journey for his master, and sign it with his master's name. If the slave were clever about it, such a paper might fool anyone who stopped to question him. Then there were slaves who just walked away from the plantation, hoping that by luck and prayer they would get to a free state. Some fugitives were caught and punished, and they never tried to run away again. Some others ran away again and again. A woman slave in North Carolina ran away sixteen times.

From the very beginning of slavery, there had been free men and women—black and white—who helped slaves to escape. George Washington said that a slave of his had been helped to escape by a group of religious people called Quakers. They had fought for many years, in their own quiet, strong way, for the freedom of the Negro. They had helped runaways to reach the North. They had set up schools for Negro children. Quakers in the South did this sort of work, as well as those in the North. In many cases, they got nothing but name-calling and abuse from their neighbors.

Working with the Quakers were the Abolitionists. The Abolitionists were men and women, black and white, who demanded freedom for the slave *now* —not little by little, not "later on," but right away. They preached freedom and traveled about in the North and Midwest getting people to join their cause. Between the Abolitionists and the Quakers, the southern plantation-owners would have had trouble enough. But add to them the great number of Negroes who had either bought their freedom, or had escaped to it. Many of these free Negroes worked with the Quakers and Abolitionists to get slaves out of the South. After 1831, when travel by steam railroad became common, the whole runaway operation became known as the Underground

Railroad. "Underground" meant out-of-sight and mysterious. "Railroad" it was, of course, because leaders, or "conductors" took "passengers" (slaves) from one "station" (friendly home) to another until a free state was reached.

Travel had to be done at night. That was the only fairly safe time. Even so, masters followed after with hounds, and there were the bounty-hunters to hide from, too. The bounty-hunters were not slave-owners, but slave-catchers. They were men who hunted down slaves for profit. They might collect the reward offered by masters, or sell the slave to someone else.

Stations were ten to fifteen miles apart—a good night's travel by foot. Once at a station, the slaves were hidden in a cellar, an attic, or the loft of a barn for the day. They ate and slept as much as they could. But sleep was not restful. For always there was the fear of being discovered, the sound of the pounding on the door, the voices:

"We are looking for two runaway slaves, ma'am. Have you seen them by any chance?"

"No, I have not."

"Would you mind if we came in and looked around all the same? Just to make sure?"

"Come in, I have nothing to hide."

Those who were hiding hardly dared to breathe. Pray the hiding place will not be found! Footsteps and voices came closer, paused, then faded away:

"Guess there's none of them here after all."

Sometimes the slaves who traveled on the Underground Railroad had to pass through dangerous swamps.

The slam of a door, and hoofbeats getting softer as the hunters-of-men rode away.

In the meantime, the people at the next "station" had received a code message. It told them to expect a certain number of escaped slaves the following morning. These secret messages traveled on what was called "the grapevine telegraph." That night, the conductor would lead the passengers through woods and swamps—any hidden place—to this next station.

There were over three thousand people actively running the Underground Railroad. They gave their time, their homes, their hearts, and their courage. Together they got 100,000 slaves out of the South between 1810 and 1850.

Most of the conductors on the Underground Railroad were men. So were most of the first slaves who escaped by it. Being a conductor was no easy task. There was the problem of getting into slave territory without being caught, of organizing a group of passengers, and of taking them to the first station, then to the next, and so on.

One of the cleverest of the white conductors was John Fairfield. His father was a slave-holder, but young John hated the very idea of slavery. He helped a slave who was his friend escape to Canada, and then came north himself. Negroes in the North soon learned of the aid he had given to his friend, and asked him to help their families and friends to escape too. So his work as a conductor began. Fairfield used a great many disguises. Sometimes he posed as a slave-holder; at other times as a slave-trader, and often as a peddler of chickens and eggs. He led large groups of slaves to Canada and freedom. Once he took a group of twenty-eight slaves. They all posed as part of a funeral procession. Fairfield was killed in 1860 during an uprising of slaves in Tennessee. He was active in the Underground Railroad right up until the very last minute of his life.

One of the greatest conductors was Harriet Tubman. She had to do a lot of talking before the leaders of the Railroad would let her become a conductor. Not only was she a woman, but she was a sickly one at that. She had been struck on the head when she was a little girl, and suffered from terrible dizzy spells ever after. In addition, she did not know how to read and write. So how could she write and read codes and maps? How could such a person bring others safely out of the South?

But Harriet knew what slavery was. She had escaped from it herself. And she had made up her mind that she was going to bring as many Negroes as she could out of that miserable life. She finally convinced the leaders of the Railroad to give her a chance.

Harriet was the best of conductors, as it turned out. Slave-owners certainly thought so. They offered $40,000 reward for her, dead or alive. Between 1850 and 1860, she went into the South nineteen

Harriet Tubman was called Moses by other Negroes. She was strong, tough, courageous, and the best conductor on the Underground Railroad.

times, and brought three hundred passengers out. Among them were her sister, her parents, and her two children.

By this time, women and children were traveling on the Underground Railroad, too. Travel was now done not only by foot, but in carts and wagons as well. The passengers often traveled by day this way, covered by hay, or other farm supplies. It was a risky business. Around 1850, the Southerners increased their efforts to break up the Underground Railroad. Runaways were chased so hard that some slaves lost courage and wanted to turn back. But Harriet would allow no turning back. If a slave suggested it, she would aim a gun at him and threaten to shoot him herself.

Harriet was tough, and she had courage. What is more, she had great faith in God. People soon began to call her *Moses*. She said, quite truly, "On my underground railroad, I never ran my train off the track, and I never lost a passenger."

Harriet proved that a blow for freedom can be struck without education. And, while she was working in her way, Negroes with education were working in theirs.

CHAPTER 4

Fighting Words

For Frederick Douglass, the wish for freedom began when he learned to read. He had been born a slave, and raised on a plantation in Maryland. When he was still a boy, he was sent to live with some of his master's relatives in Baltimore. There his new mistress, who had a small son of her own, taught Frederick to read. He learned quickly—too quickly to suit his new master, who ordered his wife to stop the lessons. It was dangerous, he said, to teach slaves to read and write. They might get "ideas." *Ideas*, of course, being ideas about freedom.

But it was too late to stop the ideas that were whirring in Frederick's head. The magic of words had caught on. There were the words *equal* and *justice* and *freedom* and *America* and *Constitution*. You could read about these ideas and a thousand other beautiful ones. And you could read about *slavery* and *injustice* and a thousand other ugly things. And you could read about what your rights were as a human being, and you could find out how to work for them.

Frederick read everything he could. He read grown-up books and newspapers, children's books and school books. He had to read them in secret of course, because if his master caught him, he would be punished. As he read, he wanted his freedom more and more, until the wish for it was like a flame inside him.

He planned his escape carefully. He used the identification papers of a sailor, and traveled, by train most of the way, to New York City. All the way along, he was in danger of being discovered as an escaped slave. Once he found himself in the same car with people whom he had known in Baltimore. Either they did not recognize him, or if they did, they pretended not to so as not to give him away.

Once he was safe in the North, he went from New York to New Bedford, Massachusetts, to work in a shipyard. And he kept on reading. One of his favorite newspapers was *The Liberator*. It was put out by a leader of the Abolitionists, a white man named William Lloyd Garrison. The paper preached brotherhood and demanded full emancipation for the slaves. Douglass listened to Garrison speak when he came to New Bedford, and said of him, "He was never loud and noisy, but calm and serene as the summer sky, and as pure."

Douglass was becoming a good speaker, too, and spoke many times in church-meeting halls. He had a beautiful, deep voice. He had educated himself by much reading, and could say things in a most intelligent way. In 1841, three years after he came to New Bedford, he was introduced to Garrison. The Abolitionist liked and admired him right away, and asked him to join their cause. Frederick did. And that was another turning point for him. He spent the rest of his life speaking and writing about freedom, about the Negro people, and about what the United States owed all its people. He established and published his own newspaper, *The North Star*. In his time, he was known as "the voice of the Negro people."

But he was far from being the only Negro voice. The years before the Civil War saw hundreds of free Negroes joining forces and speaking out for emancipation for the slaves. In 1826, *Freedom's Journal* was founded in New York City. And there were many other newspapers published by Negroes and whites who hated slavery. Not only did they fight slavery in the South, they fought inequality in the North. Although the North was a freer place than the land of plantations, there was still much prejudice and injustice in big northern cities.

In addition to the newspapers, there were books written by Negroes who had escaped from the South. Over two hundred such books were printed before the Civil War. They were widely read in the North. All the books told of conditions in the slave states —how the slave really lived, how hard he worked, how he had to face unkindness almost every day of his life. These books did much to bring the truth to Northerners. For slave-owners had tried hard to convince people that slaves were quite happy. Of course, it was rather hard to explain why so many "happy" slaves tried to escape from the plantations.

The printed word was powerful. So was the spoken word. Runaways and free Negroes spoke at many antislavery meetings in the North and West. They told of the conditions of slavery. Those who came to listen could not help but be moved by these stories of cruelty and misery.

In some towns, antislavery speakers were not allowed to rent meeting halls in which to give their talks. So, instead, they would stand on a street corner, on a porch, or under a tree. Frederick Douglass once spoke outside that way. Only five people were there to hear him at first. But soon the crowd had swelled to five hundred. People were not always friendly at these gatherings. It was not unusual for speakers to have eggs and bricks thrown at them, and there were times when speakers were injured by angry men who wanted to keep Negroes "in their place."

The Abolitionist meetings were organized by white people as well as Negroes. The Negroes themselves held many conventions in the years before the Civil War. In 1830, Negroes from New York, Pennsylvania, Maryland, Delaware, and Virginia met

Frederick Douglass, the leader of the Negro people, was also a great speaker. He traveled in America and Europe, making speeches against slavery.

30

in Philadelphia. Their purpose was to find ways of bettering the life of Negroes everywhere. They discussed raising money to build a college. In 1850 the American League of Colored Laborers came into being. Its aim was to educate Negro boys in farming, mechanics, and business. Education was an important topic at conventions in the following years. Negroes knew that unless they had skills, that unless they became educated, they would have a hard time making a living. That would give the southern whites just one more weapon. "See," they would say, "the Negro can't support himself. He's better off as a slave."

By 1860, there were four million slaves and a half million free Negroes. These free Negroes spoke for their brothers who were in bondage. When the Civil War came, free Negroes wanted to fight for their brothers, too. They had to wait. But their day was coming.

PART II

THE WAR FOR FREEDOM

CHAPTER 5

Lincoln Makes a Decision

"Peace in sixty days."

"The fewer battles the better."

That was the way the North felt when the Civil War began. No one, not even Lincoln, had any idea then that the great conflict would last for years and cost so many lives. And only the Negroes, and a few whites, believed that the war would serve to free the colored people from slavery.

For almost two years, Negroes were not allowed to join the Union Army. Lincoln kept saying that the purpose of this war was to save the Union, and not to give Negroes equal rights. But while he was saying *that*, he was *planning* something else . . . the Emancipation Proclamation.

On September 22, 1862, Lincoln announced that Liberty for millions of slaves was on the way. He said that on January 1, 1863, slaves in Confederate states—"the territory now in rebellion"—would be declared free. Slave-holders in states that were fighting with the Union could keep their slaves, or they could free them and receive money, or be compensated for each slave freed. So Lincoln was, in a way, "rewarding" slave-holders who were loyal to their country, and punishing slave-holders who were not loyal.

Negroes and other Abolitionists felt that any kind of freedom was better than none. But they were not happy about the idea of compensation for slave-owners. At a meeting where slavery was being discussed, the question was asked: "What compensation should a slave-owner receive?" A Negro in the audience answered, "The State Prison!" Nevertheless, slave-owners in Washington, D.C., received $300 for each adult set free.

Lincoln's announcement in September was a victory for the Negro people. All along they had said the war would bring freedom, and they had kept saying it even when other people shook their heads and said *no*. Yet here it was, on the way. Through the North and the Midwest, Negroes could scarcely wait for January 1. That was to be a day of triumph.

When the day came, Negroes were gathered together in meeting halls and churches. The hours dragged. The minutes dragged. Would Lincoln change his mind? Would politicians close to him convince him that Emancipation might be a poor idea? Maybe even Mrs. Lincoln would talk him into not issuing the Proclamation. After all, she came from a slave-holding family. But the word came. The Emancipation Proclamation came. Forever free, that was what the proclamation said. Slaves in Arkansas, Texas, Louisiana, Mississippi, Alabama, Florida, Georgia, South Carolina, North Carolina, and Virginia (except for West Virginia) were declared free. Approximately 3,120,000 Negroes were set free. Not all the slaves. There were still those in the border states. But most of the slaves—free forever! In the meeting halls, in the churches, there was singing, and crying, and praying, and shouting, and in some places, just the great silence that happens when people are too happy to speak.

The leaders of the Confederate states were angry beyond belief at Lincoln's announcement. Jefferson Davis, the President of the Confederacy, answered the Emancipation Proclamation by saying that all free Negroes in the South (there were 250,000 of them) would be made slaves. This threat was never carried out. Of course, the slaves in the Confederate states were not told by their masters that slavery had come to an end. They found out by the same "grapevine telegraph" that was used in the Underground Railroad. The telegraph was made of signals. The tilt of cap, to the right or to the left, meant one thing. Carrying a certain number of straws in the mouth meant something. Slaves watched to see whether their friends waved with the right or with the left hand. Such hand-signals were part of the code.

There were code names for *Lincoln*, code names

for *Union Army* and for *Confederate Army*. Often these codes were given in the form of weather reports. "They say it's going to be cloudy tomorrow" might mean that Union forces were being beaten back by the Confederates. "Sunshine on the way" might mean Union forces were coming closer. By the grapevine, the Negroes in the South found out that they were no longer slaves.

Ever since the war had begun, Negroes had left the plantations when they heard that Union forces were near. They went to the Union lines. Sometimes they had been sent back to their masters. At other times, they had been taken in and fed and clothed or given jobs building fortifications. They gave valuable information to the Union Army because they knew the areas—hills, rivers, valleys—where they lived. Now that emancipation had come true, the Negroes left the plantations in droves. They were leaving one kind of life behind. They were going into another kind of life. They did not know what to expect. The new life was going to be full of difficulties, too. But at least they were going to be free.

In the North, many white people were as happy with the proclamation as the Negroes. But many other whites were angry. They thought that free Negroes would take some of their jobs and put them out of work. "We won't fight to free the slaves," said these white laborers. In July 1863, there were riots in New York and many Negroes, children as well as adults, were injured.

But for most Northerners, the Civil War took on a new meaning because of the Emancipation Proclamation. It became a war for a great cause—a war for the whole idea of freedom. The Proclamation also had an effect on the way other countries saw the Civil War. Britain and France had at first been more in favor of the South than of the North. But with the announcement that slaves were to be freed, these two countries began to look more kindly on the northern cause.

One sentence in the Emancipation Proclamation said that freed Negroes would be used in the Union forces. The military commanders knew that the Union needed more men. Its forces had suffered terrible defeats at Bull Run, Ball's Bluff, Big Bethel, and Fredericksburg. Was the sentence put there because men were needed, or because of a real belief in equality for the Negro? It is hard to say. But with that sentence, the Negroes received another right they had been asking for—the right to serve their country and to help free their brothers in the South.

Events moved fast. In January 1863, official word was sent to Massachusetts giving that state permission to raise a Negro regiment. Frederick Douglass was to be one of the recruiting officers. In March 1863, Lincoln wrote to the Governor of Tennessee, asking him to recruit Negroes in that state. In his letter, Lincoln used almost the exact words that Frederick Douglass had used two years before:

"The bare sight of 50,000 armed and drilled black

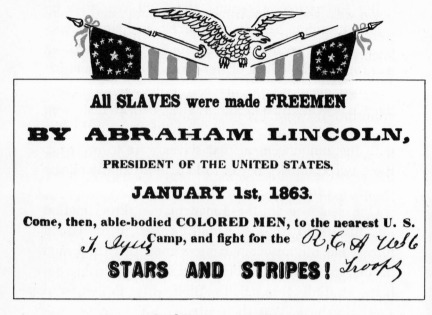

All SLAVES were made FREEMEN

BY ABRAHAM LINCOLN,

PRESIDENT OF THE UNITED STATES,

JANUARY 1st, 1863.

Come, then, able-bodied COLORED MEN, to the nearest U. S. Camp, and fight for the

STARS AND STRIPES!

A Civil War recruiting poster.

soldiers upon the banks of the Mississippi would end the rebellion at once."

On May 22, 1863, a special bureau was established in the War Department to speed up the enlistment of Negroes. The result of all the recruitment was that 180,000 Negroes served in the Union Army as fighting troops. This was a significant percentage of the Union's fighting force.

Even as a fighting man, the Negro was never fully accepted as an equal of the white soldier. To begin with, the Union Army was not integrated. There were white regiments, and there were colored regiments. The colored regiments were commanded by white officers.

At first, the Negro soldier was not even given a uniform. He wore his usual clothes, and was set to work digging and toiling in the trenches. A bit later, he was given a uniform, but it was different from the one the white soldiers wore. Then, still later, Negro soldiers were given the same uniform as whites, but they were still assigned only the "dirty" jobs, such as manning forts in areas where yellow fever often struck. Negro soldiers received less pay than white soldiers. It was seven dollars a month for Negroes, ten dollars a month for whites. Later, each group got a three-dollar raise.

Free Negroes were angry and upset at the way they were being treated as soldiers. Many of them said they would not join the Army under such unequal conditions. But Frederick Douglass urged them to enlist, angry or not. For how else were they to prove themselves as brave and intelligent soldiers? "Men of Color, To Arms!" became Douglass' rallying cry. He said to every Negro to "Get an eagle on his button, a musket on his shoulder, and the Star-Spangled Banner over his head," for "Liberty won by white men would lose half its luster."

This was the hour. The gate of the prison stood open.

CHAPTER 6

A Brave Black Regiment

The first state permitted to raise a Negro regiment was Massachusetts. Douglass and the other recruiting officers went all over that state, and to other states, getting colored men to enlist. Massachusetts did not have enough colored men to make up a complete regiment. Douglass' sons, Charles and Lewis, were the first Negroes from New York to join the Massachusetts group. Eventually there were two regiments, the Massachusetts 54th and 55th. Like other Negro regiments from other parts of the country, they proved themselves to be good soldiers. The Massachusetts 54th, in fact, made such a brilliant record for courage that few white regiments could claim to be better.

The commanding officer of the 54th was Colonel Robert Gould Shaw, a young white man of a well-known northern family. His family had come from Massachusetts, where his grandfather had been a leading Abolitionist. The other officers were white, too. From the very beginning there seems to have been no prejudice, no hate, no bad feelings at all

Colonel Robert G. Shaw, Commander of 54th Massachusetts Regiment, was killed in the battle of Fort Wagner on July 17, 1863. (Culver Pictures, Inc.)

A Negro soldier in the Union Army in 1863.

between the Negro soldiers and their officers. The officers expected the best from their men, and they got it. At Fort Wagner near Charleston, South Carolina, Negro courage was tested, and proved.

Wagner was a strong, well-manned Confederate fort on the seacoast of South Carolina. In July 1863, the 54th's orders were to spearhead an attack on the fort. Following the 54th would be other regiments (white). The fort had been bombarded from the harbor for a few days. It was thought that the defenses were probably weakened. Still, the soldiers knew that the task before them was going to be very difficult. Here they were, a mere six hundred men, without sleep for three days, and without food for two. Defending the fort were seventeen hundred men, protected by a strong earthwork fort.

To capture that fort—that was the task that faced the Massachusetts 54th. The officers' thoughts were with their men. Would the men behave bravely? Would they advance in the face of gunfire? Or would they turn coward and run away? The whole question of using colored soldiers in the Union Army depended upon the way the 54th acted on this warm July night. "Now I want you to prove yourselves," said Colonel Shaw as they waited in the twilight for the order to attack. The waiting was almost unbearable. Finally the signal to advance came. Colonel Shaw gave the command "Attention!" The men sprang to their feet. "Move in quick time until within a hundred yards of the fort; then double quick, and charge!" and the 54th advanced to the storming.

It was about seven forty-five in the evening when the order came. Darkness fell rapidly. Three-quarters of a mile of beach had to be crossed be-

The 54th Massachusetts Regiment at the Battle of Fort Wag-
ner, near Charleston, South Carolina, July 1863.

fore the men reached the fort. When the 54th was two hundred yards from its goal, the Confederates let loose with shot and shell. The 54th was bombarded with what seemed to be a sheet of flame, and men fell on every side. But there was no stop or pause in the 54th's advance. The only change was that they quickened their pace and moved more rapidly toward the enemy. The officers rode to the front, and the men set their jaws, lowered their heads, and pushed forward. Closer and closer they came. Confederate soldiers continued their fire, and Union men continued to fall. Finally only a huge ditch separated the 54th from the enemy. Sergeant William H. Carney, a Negro of Company C, was the standard-bearer. He carried the nation's flag up the ditch and planted it on the parapet of the fort. He had been wounded twice already in this fierce battle, but as he said later, "The old flag never touched the ground!"

Colonel Shaw was always in front of his men. He got to the rampart, and stood there, with sword uplifted. His men heard him shout, "Forward, Fifty-fourth!" Then he fell dead, shot through the heart.

Several other officers were severely wounded; and hundreds of soldiers had already fallen before the fort was reached. Those who got into the fort were too few in number to hold it. Wagner was stronger and better defended than the Union had guessed. The 54th was pushed back, wounded and dying, into the night. They continued to fight. But the charge

Sergeant William H. Carney, Company C, 54th Massachusetts Regiment. Received the Congressional Medal of Honor for heroism at the battle of Fort Wagner.
(Culver Pictures, Inc.)

49

had been made and defeated before any other Union troops arrived. When supporting troops did come, they too were pushed back with heavy losses. The Confederate loss was 181 men killed or wounded. The Union's loss was 1515, including 111 officers.

Wagner was one of the fiercest struggles of the war. The bravery of the 54th Massachusetts was noted by Union and Confederate writers alike. On July 19, the day after the battle, a reporter for the New York *Herald* said, "I saw them fight at Wagner as none but splendid soldiers, splendidly officered, could fight, dashing through shot and shell, grape, canister, and shrapnel, and showers of bullets, and when they got close enough, fighting with clubbed muskets, and retreating when they did retreat, by command."

A Confederate lieutenant, Iredell Jones, wrote: "I visited the battery (Fort Wagner) yesterday. The dead and wounded were piled up in a ditch together sometimes fifty in a heap, and they were strewn all over the plain for a distance of three-fourths of a mile. One pile of Negroes numbered thirty. Numbers of both white and black were killed on top of our breastworks as well as inside. The Negroes fought gallantly, and were lead by as brave a colonel as ever lived. He mounted the breastworks waving his sword, and at the head of his regiment, and he and a Negro orderly sergeant fell dead over

Miles Moore, musician, Company H, 54th Massachusetts Regiment.

the inner crest of the works. The Negroes were as fine-looking a set as I ever saw—large, strong, muscular fellows."

While a few Confederates, like Lieutenant Jones, may have had some admiration for the 54th, most Confederates felt that the idea of a black regiment was shameful. Negro soldiers were fighting white men! White officers were actually leading these Negroes into battle! How dare they! To show how they felt about white officers leading colored troops, the Confederates stripped the dead Colonel Shaw of his uniform. This was against the rule of military courtesy. An officer's body should be treated with respect, regardless of whose side he had been fighting on, and the body was supposed to be returned to friends. But Shaw's body was thrown into a ditch with dead colored soldiers, and they were all covered over with earth.

By burying Shaw with Negroes, the Confederates meant to insult him and his family. But Shaw's family took it as an honor. The following month, when Union troops finally occupied Wagner, the soldiers began a search for Shaw's grave. They hoped they could send his body back to New York for burial. When he heard of the search, Shaw's father wrote a letter to the commanding officer and asked him not to disturb the grave. Said Mr. Shaw, "A soldier's most appropriate burial-place is on the field where he has fallen. . . . I shall therefore be much obliged if you will prevent the disturbance of his remains or those buried with him."

Perhaps Colonel Shaw's death was more merciful than the one he might have had if he had been captured alive by the Confederates. In May 1863 the Confederate Congress had passed an act which said that any white man who led or trained Negro troops to fight against Confederate troops would, if captured, be put to death or "otherwise punished." *Otherwise punished* meant torture.

Torture may have been the way several captured Negro soldiers of the 54th met their deaths. Of the sixty taken by Confederates, twenty were already wounded. Some of the other forty were killed by their captors. And some of the prisoners were sold into slavery. This too was a violation of the rules of war, a violation so terrible that on July 30, 1863, Abraham Lincoln issued a proclamation. It did something to bring equal rights to Negro prisoners, if not to Negro soldiers. The proclamation began:

"It is the duty of every government to give protection to its citizens of whatever class, color, or condition, and especially to those who are duly organized as soldiers in the public service." The proclamation ended with this paragraph:

"It is therefore ordered that for every soldier of the United States killed in violation of the laws of war, a Rebel soldier shall be executed, and for every one enslaved by the enemy or sold into slavery, a

Rebel soldier shall be placed at hard labor on the public works, and continue at such labor until the other shall be released and receive the treatment due a prisoner of war."

This strong statement of Lincoln's did help to stop the Confederate abuse of Negro prisoners and their white officers captured in battle.

That was one benefit to come out of the 54th's battle at Fort Wagner. But more important, the Negro had proved himself to be a soldier who could face danger as well as any man could. The soldiers of the 54th were gallant warriors. From that time on, Negroes were sent into battle more often, and were given jobs that suited their courage and willingness to fight.

CHAPTER 7

Many Ways of Serving

Glory came to the Negro on the battlefield. And it came to the Negro who was not in uniform. The hard-working Frederick Douglass was an example. After the battle at Fort Wagner, he went to see President Lincoln at the White House. In the busy and tragic days of the War, Lincoln could not see everyone who wanted to talk to him. Many had been turned away. But Douglass was special, and the President welcomed him.

Douglass was bothered by the way Negro soldiers had been treated when they were captured by Confederate forces. He felt that perhaps Lincoln's proclamation of July 30 was not strong enough. The South would still not exchange Negro prisoners for white ones held by the North. There were reports that though Negro prisoners were not being shot, they were still being tortured. Perhaps the South would listen if Lincoln said that southern soldiers would be tortured, and would not be exchanged.

Douglass also asked Lincoln why Negroes could not receive a commission (become officers), and why their pay was still lower than that of white soldiers. Until these things were equalized, said Douglass, he felt he could not go on recruiting young Negro men to join the army.

This first meeting between the two leaders was a strange one. The men liked each other right away, but they did not agree on many things. Lincoln was as shocked as Douglass was by the treatment Negroes received at the hands of their southern captors. But he could not bring himself to promise torture in return. As Douglass thought of this later, he wrote:

"I saw the tender heart of a man rather than the stern warrior and commander-in-chief of the American army and navy, and while I could not agree with him, I could but respect his humane spirit."

As far as equal pay was concerned, Lincoln had a go-slow policy on that. The big step, he said, had been made. The very fact that Negroes were *in* the army was a great breakthrough. He was afraid that giving them equal pay would simply anger the white soldiers. Lincoln was aware that there was plenty of prejudice in the North. The Emancipation Proclamation hadn't changed that.

The President said he would certainly give commissions to Negroes who were recommended to him by the Secretary of War. Douglass knew the Secretary was a fair man, so he had to be satisfied with

A meeting between President Lincoln and Frederick Douglass at the White House—1863. Douglass asked for equal pay for Negro soldiers and better treatment of Negro prisoners held by the Confederates.

that. This was the only point of agreement. But Douglass left the White House promising to go on with his recruiting. A friendship had begun, and there were to be other meetings.

And Douglass' wish for a stronger stand on treatment of prisoners was going to come true, too. It was going to come to pass because of a tragic event.

On April 12, 1864, there were over five hundred Union men stationed at Fort Pillow, in Tennessee. Most of them were Negro, and some had brought their wives and children along to live at the Fort. The other men were Tennessee whites who had sided with the Union.

Confederate soldiers hated the whole arrangement at Fort Pillow. First of all there were Negroes in uniform! There were whites fighting beside them! And these were whites who were supposed to be loyal Southerners. The Confederates longed to attack. And on that April day they did. They overran the Fort, shouting "No quarter" (which means "no mercy"), and killed everyone in sight. Women and children were not spared. Fort Pillow became a scene of blood and tears and terror.

The attack on the fort acted like a shock-wave as the news traveled through the North. It made Union soldiers, especially the Negro ones, fight with new strength and fierceness. Lincoln at last made it clear to the South that unless captured Negroes were exchanged for captured Confederates, there would be no exchange at all. As for torture of Negro troops or their officers, if this continued, southern prisoners would meet the same fate. Frederick Douglass had been proved right again.

Negroes were gaining respect in countless numbers of ways. About 180,000 of them worked with the Union forces as cooks and as teamsters. They helped to build fortifications. Many Negroes went behind enemy lines to do dangerous work as spies. Others helped Yankees to escape from Confederate prisons. Harriet Tubman, who had worked so hard on the Underground Railroad, was now a nurse with the Union forces.

There had never been any problem about the Negro finding a place in the United States Navy. He had been there, since the time of the American Revolution. Negroes made up one-fourth of the manpower of the Navy. There were, though, the same old inequalities of pay.

Some Negroes who were forced to work with the Confederate Navy performed great acts of heroism for the Union. Robert Smalls, for instance, managed to slip a Confederate vessel through to the Union side. William Tillman overpowered a whole crew to bring his ship to the northern forces.

As time came around for a new Presidential election, the skies looked clearer for the North and for the Negro. Union General McClellan had been replaced by General Ulysses S. Grant. He willingly used colored troops, and commanded his white troops to treat them with respect. Grant was an excellent general, and soon had Virginia in his control. Union General William T. Sherman was marching across Georgia to the sea. The Democrats said the war was not going well, and had chosen General McClellan as their candidate to run against Lincoln. But with Union victories increasing, Lincoln was sure of re-election.

Frederick Douglass attended Lincoln's Second Inaugural Ball. His friends had tried to talk him out of going. "You'll simply be turned away at the door," they said. "They won't let Negroes in." And this did almost happen. The people tending the door at the President's home tried to turn Douglass away. But he managed to send word to Lincoln that he was there, and then Lincoln himself came forward, with hands extended, and greeted Douglass, and led him in to meet the other people gathered there. It was the first time that a Negro had been welcomed at the Great Ball. That kind of thing had "never been done" before.

Douglass said later, "I have found that the way to break down an unreasonable custom is to contradict it in practice."

The "custom" of believing that the Negro had no courage. The "custom" of believing that the Negro had no brains. These and other "customs" were being broken down as the war drew into its last days.

CHAPTER 8

The Negro in the South

It took the Union almost two years to decide that the Negro could serve the war effort as well as any white man. But, from the very beginning of the War, the Confederate Army had forced the Negro to serve the southern cause. Negroes on the plantations grew and harvested food for the army. Others were taken from plantations, often against the wishes of their masters, and had to do the hard and dirty work of the war. They built fortifications and trenches. They worked in field hospitals. All this was slave labor, of course. In the early days of the war, it helped the Confederate Army immensely. For white soldiers were able to spend their time in actual fighting. Whites did not have to stay behind to grow food and do other un-glorious work.

So most of the young white southern men went off to battle. This left women, children, and old men in charge of the plantations and farms. How easy it would have been for the slaves to overpower these weaker masters, kill them, and run away! But, to the Negro's credit, he did not take advantage of the

When they heard that the Union Army was near, large numbers of Negro slaves walked from the plantations into the Union camps.

weakness of the people left to "guard" him. When the Negro struck, it was usually because he had been cruelly mistreated, just as in the days before the war.

But this does not mean that all the Negro slaves continued to work on the plantations. As soon as they heard that Union troops were near, many Negroes put down their hoes and shovels, and went to the Union camps. Slave-owners had been afraid that just this very thing might happen. They had set up patrols to spot and capture runaway slaves. But the patrols found it almost impossible to carry out this assignment. It was like trying to hold back the tides of the ocean. The tide goes out, no matter what.

The Negroes who came to the Union camps were usually given some protection. The men were of great use around the camp, helping the soldiers. But the Union officers were really at a loss when it came to feeding all the new arrivals, caring for the women and children, finding them a place to sleep, and getting them clothing to wear. Army camps were just not able to care for all these civilians. In many cases, Negroes suffered real hardship. Without proper housing, they were exposed to cold rains and chilling winds. There was sickness and hunger.

People in the North saw a problem taking shape in the South. The problem was Freedom, that great good thing that good men had fought for so long and hard. Freedom was almost won. Now Negroes could leave the plantations where they had so long been slaves. But when they left the plantations, they also left the hut, the food, and the clothing (poor as it all was). Freedom was going to have to supply these same things—food, clothing, homes. For Freedom is sweet, but so is food and a place to lay your head.

Seeing the problem, Northerners began to send help to Negroes in Union camps in the South. Food came, clothing came, people came to help build shelters. Teachers began to come and set up schools. But the help was scattered. Money was scarce. Everyone knew that the help was going to have to be better organized. Maybe the United States Government would help. Maybe, when the war was over . . .

And the grim, hard years of war *were* almost over. The winter of 1864–1865 was a season of southern defeats. The Union Army won victory after victory. Slave-owners saw fate moving in. Some of them ran away from their own plantations as the Union troops approached. One Negro happily advertised for his "Runaway Master." He offered a reward of $500.

That winter, the Union was caught up in a feeling of triumph. On February 1, 1865, the United States Congress wrote and voted to adopt the 13th Amendment. This Amendment was to give freedom to *all* slaves forever. The Emancipation Proclamation had been an executive order—an order of the President made in the emergency of war. The 13th Amendment was different, however. As soon as the individual states ratified, or *approved*, it, the Amendment would become part of the United States Constitution. Then it would be a law, and good for all time:

1) Neither slavery nor involuntary servitude, except as a punishment for crime whereof the party shall have been duly convicted, shall exist within the United States, or any place subject to their jurisdiction.

2) Congress shall have the power by appropriate legislation, to enforce the provisions of this article.

Lincoln was so pleased with this amendment that he signed his name to it, although the Supreme Court had ruled many years before that the President need not have anything to do with the amendments to the Constitution.

Two days later, on February 3, the Confederate Government asked the Union to work out peace terms. By now, with defeat closing in, the southern states were ready to give up the idea of being a separate nation. If you want peace, said Lincoln, you will have to accept the 13th Amendment. This the South refused to do. So the war was to drag on for two more months. More men had to die.

In the South, casualties were heavy. More soldiers were needed. And so the Confederates, who had cried "Shame!" when the Union made colored men soldiers, decided to use Negro soldiers too. On March 13, 1865, Jefferson Davis, the President of the Confederacy, approved the raising of 300,000 Negro troops. General Robert E. Lee, the Commander of the

Confederate Army, approved the idea. But he said that if Negroes were going to fight, they would have to be given their freedom.

Many Southerners were deathly afraid of using Negro soldiers. What would they do with guns and bayonets in their hands? Perhaps they would turn on the southern whites.

This great experiment, this test of using Negroes to fight *for* the slave-owners, never had a chance to be tried out. Before the troops could be raised, the war was over. On April 9, 1865, at Appomattox Court House in Virginia, General Lee surrendered to General Grant. Among the Union troops at Appomattox there were thousands of Negro soldiers. They were tired and worn and had seen the terror of war. They were ready to lay down their guns at last. The War for Freedom was won.

But other kinds of battles lay ahead.

CHAPTER 9

Glory Enough for a Day

At the end of the Civil War, the Negro soldier had the right to hold his head as high as any man's. Higher, maybe. When all was told, Negro soldiers had been given the hardest kind of camp work, the poorest equipment, the worst medical care. Yet they had taken part in two hundred battles. In many of the most dangerous battles, Negro troops had been sent first into the fire, as at Fort Wagner. To spearhead an attack this way meant many deaths. Altogether, 36,000 Negro soldiers were killed in the Civil War.

Negro soldiers conducted themselves like true heroes. Their war record was a proud one. They gained the admiration and respect of officers and civilians, too.

Four Negroes received the Navy Medal of Honor.

Fourteen Negroes were awarded the Congressional Medal of Honor for heroic conduct on the field of battle.

Abraham Lincoln said that if the Negro troops had been taken from the Union side, then the Union would have been forced to abandon the war.

A Negro soldier being decorated. Fourteen Negroes received the Congressional Medal of Honor for heroism on the battlefield. Many others received medals for gallantry and service beyond the call of duty.

Listen:

To a commander of Negro troops: "They are attentive and enthusiastic, eager to take the field and be led into action."

To a white general: "When the Negroes first came to the camps, they tended to look down at the ground as if they were slaves. After a while, they began to straighten themselves, throw back their shoulders, stand erect, and very soon look God straight in the face."

To a newspaper reporter who saw one of the first battles in which Negroes fought, near Butler, Missouri: "It is useless to talk about Negro courage. The men fought like tigers."

At the end of the war, these brave men could rejoice at freedom with a special kind of pride. For they had helped to win it.

Now victory was achieved. And joy filled the heart of every Negro, whether soldier or civilian. There was prayer, and shouting, and singing.

"I feel all right for the first time in my life," said one old man.

In meeting halls and churches, Negroes and whites sang "John Brown's Body" and "The Star-Spangled Banner." But the Negroes sang with such great feeling, that the whites stopped their own singing to listen to this, the voice of freedom.

Even little children seemed to know what freedom meant. Some Negro youngsters were asked, "Is that your mother over there in the ditch?"

"Yes," they said sadly.

"Is she dead?"

"She's dead, but she's free," said the children.

In Richmond, Virginia, once a stronghold of the slave-owners, freed men and women saw President

Lincoln. Nobody had expected the President. He came there unannounced. There he was, tall, thin, tired. The Negroes recognized him immediately, and rushed forward to greet him. He was deeply moved by all the thanks extended to him.

"God bless you, Mr. Lincoln," many of them said.

Someone said, "I know I'm free, for I have seen Father Abraham."

And Lincoln answered:

"Let me say God has made you free. Although you have been deprived of your God-given rights by your so-called masters, you are now as free as I am, and if those that claim to be your superiors do not know that you are free, take the sword and bayonet and teach them that you are . . . for God created all men free, giving to each the same rights of life, liberty and the pursuit of happiness."

Less than a week later, Lincoln was assassinated. On April 14, while watching a play at Ford's Theater in Washington, the President was shot by an actor named John Wilkes Booth. Lincoln struggled for life for a few hours, but by the following day the struggle was over.

When a President dies, it is like a death in the family. And when the President was a good and strong man, the shock is almost too much to bear. For Negroes the shock was double. Here was the man who had helped them through the war. They had expected him to help them through the peace, too. What would become of them, now that their friend was dead? And what would become of the nation which needed to be joined together again in peace?

So, among Negroes, there was a moment of fear. Then they gathered their courage, remembered their new freedom, and faced the future with determination.

CHAPTER 10

Freedom Sings

Song can express all kinds of feelings. People sing when they are unhappy, and they sing when they are happy. They sing when they have reached a great goal, and they sing when they are years away from that goal.

The songs the Negroes sang before the war, during the war, and after the war show us something of their emotions and thoughts at these different times.

One thing was certain—the songs that slaves sang on the plantations were not songs of happiness. Sometimes the slave-owners tried to pretend they were: "How can you say that my slaves are miserable?" he might say to a visiting Northerner. "Listen to them singing. Would they be singing if they were miserable?"

The answer to that was "Yes." Here is what Frederick Douglass said in his book about his days as a slave:

"The songs of the slave represent the sorrows of his heart; and he is relieved by them, only as an aching heart is relieved by its tears. At least, such is my experience. I have often sung to drown my sorrows, but seldom to express my happiness. Crying for joy, and singing for joy were alike uncommon to me while in the jaws of slavery."

The songs sung on the plantations often seemed quite harmless to the outsider, whether these songs were sad or happy. They were mostly spirituals, songs about God, heaven, and the wish for restful death. Or at least that is what the songs *seemed* to be about. Many of them really contained coded messages. The messages urged Negroes to come to secret meetings, or gave escape routes to the North.

Many of the songs expressed just plain anger. They might be sung in a slow and peaceful way, but if the slave-owner ever stopped and really listened to the words, he might have been stunned by what he heard. One of the angriest songs went simply:

> Oh Freedom, Oh Freedom,
> Oh Freedom, Lord, for me,
> And before I'd be a slave
> I'd be buried in my grave
> Go home to my Lord and be free.

What more did the slave-owner need to tell him that his slaves were truly unhappy, and were going to fight for their freedom some day? After all, the song *did* say that the Negro would rather die than continue being a slave.

This same song became a marching song for Negro

The slaves sang many songs which showed how much they hated slavery and longed for freedom.

troops during the Civil War. The tone of it had changed a little, though. Maybe there was a note of triumph in it. When the war had ended, "Oh Freedom" became a cry of victory.

That particular song, of course, has never died out. Fifty-five years ago there was a race riot in Atlanta, Georgia, and afterward, thousands of Negroes marched through the city streets singing it. Nowadays, the song is still sung. It has become a song to give people courage, and a song to make them work together for a common cause. The song, and the cause, are still the same. They are about Freedom.

Many songs that began as "Negro songs" became everybody's song. That was true of the song "John Brown's Body." Negro troops in the Civil War made it one of their favorites, for it told about the man who had struck a blow for freedom before the war ever started.

John Brown's body lies a'moulderin' in the grave,
But his soul goes marching on.

Later, the song was given new words by Julia Ward Howe, and became "The Battle Hymn of the Republic." It was a Union Army song now, and a song of triumph:

Mine eyes have seen the glory
Of the coming of the Lord.

Negro spirituals and church songs were again

used many years later, when men and women were trying to get better working conditions. Negro and white workers alike took "We Are Climbing Jacob's Ladder" and made it into "We Are Building a Strong Union." Today we sing it as "Do you, do you want your freedom?"

If there is any song today that is thought of as being *the* freedom song, it is "We Shall Overcome." The song brings the people and their leaders together, and singing it gives a certain strength. Labor unions used it during the 1940s. Negro members of the Food and Tobacco Workers Association in Charleston, South Carolina, sang it in a picket line in 1946. But they changed the words to *"We will* overcome . . ."

The song showed up again during the Montgomery, Alabama, bus boycott in December 1955. It has never faded away.

We can learn much about a group of people and their condition by listening to their music.

Part III

FREE AT LAST

CHAPTER 11

New Beginnings and New Problems

So here was the Negro at the end of the war. He was free at last. The world seemed a brighter place, a place full of possibilities for himself and for his children. He had been through a trial of fire—a great war—and he had come out a winner. This gave him a sense of self-respect. He looked at himself as a new man. He might take a new name, or at least a last name (which slaves had never had). He wanted to be addressed courteously as *Mr.*, and have his wife and daughters addressed as *Mrs.* or *Miss.*

The Negro was also eager to work for pay, so that he could keep his own home and buy his own food and clothing. He wanted to learn to read and write. He wanted to be part of the community. Above all, he wanted to own land to farm. But it was going to take some time before the new, free man could get these things. For freedom had brought problems as well as blessings.

The South was now a war-torn land. Everything was in confusion. Some farms and plantations had been deserted. Others had been destroyed. Thousands of people, white and black, had become wanderers. As Frederick Douglass saw it, the Negro was "free at last from the plantation, but had only the dusty road under his feet." He had no money, no property. He had lost some powerful friends, too. For, with freedom won, many Abolitionists thought their work was finished. Fortunately the Negro gained a new "friend." The friend was a government organization called the Freedmen's Bureau.

The Bureau was founded in March 1865. It grew out of the work that had been done for southern Negroes by private individuals during the war. The Bureau's job was to help solve the problems that Negroes faced. Many were homeless, sick, and hungry. The Freedmen's Bureau found homes for those who had none. Hospitals were set up, and medicine was distributed. Food was given out. White people who needed help also came to the Bureau.

The Bureau had many enemies. In the North, some people thought the whole operation was too expensive. War had cost untold millions. People were not willing to spend as much for peace. Most white Southerners hated the Bureau because it was helping the Negro. Also the Bureau was started by the Republican Party, which was then in power. Most Southerners were Democrats, and so the whites thought that the Freedmen's Bureau might start a strong Republican feeling in the South.

Something else was bothering the southern whites, too. It was more than the food and medicine being handed out. It was more than politics. It was the other work that the Bureau was doing—the work for the future. For the Bureau was doing more than relieving present pain. It was helping the ex-slave to build a good free life in the years to come—just as good a life as the white man had. That was a bitter pill for the southern whites.

The Freedmen's Bureau saw to it that Negroes got paying jobs. Work contracts were arranged between employer and employee. The Bureau made sure that both kept the agreement. This meant that men and women who used to be slaves, who used to work for nothing, now had to be paid wages. This was pretty hard for the old masters to take. But, if they wanted their farms planted, and tilled, and harvested, they had no choice.

It was not only the farm-owners who objected to the Negro working for money. The poor white laborer didn't like it, either. For now he thought of the Negro as someone he had to fight to get a job. The white laborer might have looked at it another way. He might have seen that the greater the free labor force, the more powerful it is. And the more powerful it is, the more good things it can get for all laborers. The white laborer might have seen, too, that when the Negro had been a slave-laborer, the white laborer

During Reconstruction, for the first time large numbers of Negroes were paid for their work. The Freedmen's Bureau helped Negroes get jobs.

couldn't get a job on a farm at all. For what owner would hire a man for money when he could get a slave to do the job for nothing?

When Negroes won their freedom, they really won something for the white man, too. They gave the white man a chance to get more work, work that hadn't been open to him before the war. But the white working man didn't see things that way. He, too, was poor. And the powerful white Southerners encouraged him in his beliefs. In that way, they could keep all the whites on one side, against the Negro.

The Freedmen's Bureau went on adding fuel to the angry white fire. Freedmen's courts were set up, so that the Negro could be sure of being treated fairly by the law. Schools were established for young and old alike. The most educated and most devoted school teachers came down from the North to help. They trained Negro teachers in the South. They taught reading and writing and they also taught skills, such as carpentry and weaving and building, to prepare the students to earn a living. The love of learning, which Frederick Douglass had first felt so many years before, spread into almost every nook and cranny in the southern states.

One of the greatest needs that the Negro had was the need for land. The ideal life for many seemed to be one in which they could own and run a small farm. Like so many other Americans, the Negro was a man of the soil. He longed for cheap land, free land. In 1862 the Federal Government had begun to give 160 acres to anyone who would settle and develop it. Most of the land being offered was in the West. The Negro wanted his land in the South. That was his home, in spite of everything. He asked for forty acres there, and a mule. The request seemed small enough.

The Freedmen's Bureau began to help him get this land. Farms that had been abandoned, farms that had been taken away from southern planters—some of these lands were sold to Negroes. Some 485,000 acres were divided in this way among 40,000 Negroes. For these people, a bright dream seemed to be coming true. They began to work the land, free farmers in a free land.

But the dream was shattered. Before long, the plantation-owners were pardoned. They took their land back. The Negroes who worked it were chased off.

CHAPTER 12

Some Problems Solved

White Southerners were stunned and angry at the terrible defeat they had suffered in the war. They had been set back for a moment. But they quickly got together and decided that they would continue ruling the South. They were determined not to let the newly freed Negro and the northern politicians have anything to say about governing the southern states.

So when Congress met in December 1865, the South sent all her old leaders back to Washington. These were men who had led the Confederacy in its fight against the Union. But these men were not admitted to Congress.

Many Northerners were enraged to see the Confederate leaders still in power. Abolitionists and northern Republicans thought the South should be punished for its rebellion. And there was a great fear that these southern leaders would put the Negro back into a condition very near slavery.

A powerful group of Northerners, led by Thad-

85

deus Stevens, proposed two bills in Congress. One bill would keep the Freedmen's Bureau in the South for many years. The second bill would guarantee the Negro his Civil Rights. These bills, Stevens hoped, would give the Negro a chance to become a successful, important part of southern life. The Stevens group also proposed a new amendment to the Constitution. This amendment, the 14th, would make the Negro a citizen.

The new President, Andrew Johnson, was against all these measures. He thought the Freedmen's Bureau was too expensive. Besides, said Johnson, it was doing more for the Negro than it was for the white man! As for Civil Rights and citizenship, the Negro was not "ready" for these things yet. The President would rather leave these matters to the southern states to decide.

The Civil Rights bill passed through Congress anyway. But the South ignored it completely. Instead of giving the Negro rights, southern politicians began to take them away. They enacted Black Codes to "keep the Negro in his place." One code stated that Negroes could not be given licenses to do skilled jobs (such as carpentry). Another code kept the Negro from going to other areas to look for work. Still another said that Negroes who were caught wandering homeless and out of a job would be put to work on plantations, without pay. The South

The South enacted the Black Codes to put the Negro in his place. According to some people the Negro's place was on the plantation, working without pay.

said these codes were necessary to "keep order" in the South.

Nevertheless, the South continued to be a place of great disorder. Southern leaders refused to accept the 14th Amendment. President Johnson agreed with them, and northern leaders grew increasingly angry.

What is this amendment that aroused so much argument? It is one that states just who an American citizen is: 1) a person who is born in the United States, or 2) a person who is *naturalized,* that is, a person who comes here from another country and passes certain citizenship tests. Most of the Negroes in the United States at that time had been born here. So, according to the 14th Amendment, they were citizens.

Just as important, the 14th Amendment said that an American was not only a citizen of a state, he was a citizen of the *United States.* The nation would protect his rights. The first part of the amendment reads:

All persons born or naturalized in the United States and subject to the jurisdiction thereof, are citizens of the United States and of the State wherein they reside. No State shall make or enforce any law which shall abridge the privileges or immunities of citizens of the United States, nor shall any State deprive any person of life, liberty or property without due process of law, nor deny to any person within its jurisdiction the equal protection of the laws.

There was much hatred in the nation in those days. The North hated the South "for causing the war." The South hated the North "for causing the war." It is strange that anything good at all could come out of so much bad feeling. But the 14th Amendment, in its definition of a citizen and its promise to protect him, was a good thing. It helped not only the Negro, but all the people who were coming to the United States from other countries to live and work and make their homes. They were to become *naturalized* citizens.

Another section of the amendment stated that any person who had held an important political office before the war and then had joined the Confederacy could no longer take part in the government. This meant that nearly all southern politicians would be out of work.

It is not hard to see why the southern whites were against this amendment. It would remove all power from their leaders. And that was what Thaddeus Stevens wanted to do—that, and take away some of the President's power and give that power back to Congress. The Stevens committee next presented to Congress some bills which would become the Reconstruction Act of 1867. The Act said:

1) States that had been part of the Confederacy were to be divided into five military districts. These districts would be ruled by the Army. Tennessee was the only exception. That state was carrying out its own reconstruction in a successful way.

2) All loyal male adults, regardless of race, were to be allowed to vote.

3) Each state was to make a state constitution that was acceptable to Congress.

4) No state could come back into the Union unless it passed the 14th Amendment.

5) Southerners who had rebelled against the Union would not be allowed to vote.

President Johnson vetoed the act. He said it was unfair to the southern states. And he said that the Negroes hadn't asked for the franchise (the right to vote). In this he was wrong. For many years, Negroes such as Frederick Douglass had been saying that the Negro should be a *full* citizen. And citizenship includes the franchise.

Congress passed the Reconstruction Act over President Johnson's veto. It was a great victory for Congress, because Congress seemed to be more powerful than the President. The Reconstruction Act was passed during troubled times, and there were going to be bad things resulting from it—hard feelings, dishonesty, and battles for power. But Reconstruction was also going to offer many bright good things for the Negro and for the nation.

CHAPTER 13

This Land Is My Land

The 14th Amendment made the Negro a citizen. The Reconstruction Act demanded that this new citizen be given the franchise, the right to vote. But the Negro franchise would never be a permanent part of United States law until it also was written as an amendment to the Constitution.

Frederick Douglass called the franchise the "one great power by which all civil rights are obtained." For it is one thing to be a citizen and *expect* certain rights to be given to you. But it is a more powerful thing to vote for the men who will help you to get these rights. Negroes in the North and in the South worked for an amendment that would guarantee them the franchise for all time.

At first, Negroes met an almost solid wall of opposition. Even some of the Abolitionists were against the Negro franchise. William Lloyd Garrison, the Abolitionist leader, did not immediately like the idea. Along with many others, he felt the southern Negro was not educated enough to use this right wisely. And he felt that the franchise would increase the bad feelings between white and colored peoples in the South. Douglass was patient with his old friend. Said Douglass, "A man's head will not long remain wrong when his heart is right."

Douglass also realized that the franchise *would* result in increased bad feeling in the South. But he felt the Negro's future would be even worse if he were left in the "care" of his old masters. Douglass agreed, too, that the southern Negro was uneducated. Slavery had kept him so. But he knew the franchise would help open the schoolhouse door to him. Negroes, always eager to learn, would certainly vote for more and better schools for the common people, white as well as Negro.

President Johnson was also opposed to the Negro franchise. In February 1866, Douglass and other Negro leaders met with Johnson to tell him their views. But the President would not listen. So Douglass had the Negro view published in sympathetic newspapers. He did a good job of presenting both sides of the case.

Johnson had said that the southern Negro hated the poor whites in the South. It was from the poor white class that the overseers, slave-catchers, and slave-drivers had come. The President believed that if the Negro got the vote, he would use it to punish the poor whites. Well, said Douglass, the Negro *did* hate the poor white in the days of slavery.

But now the freed Negro was eager to look ahead to the future, not back to the past.

Besides, if the President believed that the poor whites and the Negro were enemies, why should he give the poor white political power (the vote) and strip the Negro of all political power? Wasn't this putting the Negro at the mercy of his former enemy?

Johnson had looked for a way out of his troublesome situation. He had suggested *colonization* for the Negro. That is, he suggested that the Government help the Negro go to other countries to live— countries in Africa, perhaps, or island-countries in the Caribbean, or nations in Latin America. Colonization had been suggested many times before the Civil War. Douglass and his followers found it an especially ignorant suggestion now. For the Negro had proved himself a good worker, a fine soldier, and a loyal American. No matter what hardships come to a man, the land where he grew up, the land of his birth, remains *his* country and his home. He wants to stay there, and work to make it a better home.

Johnson objected to the franchise, but the Negroes went to their friend in the Senate. He was Senator Charles Sumner from Massachusetts. Sumner took up the battle for the Negro's right to vote. The answer Sumner got at first was that all Negroes would soon die, since they were starving to death in the South, so the franchise was unnecessary. Dead men can't vote!

But soon the Senate began to think about the situation more kindly. They proposed an amendment which said:

The southern states could decide who was to vote and who was not to vote.

If all adult males were allowed to vote, that state could send its full number of representatives to Congress.

If some adult males were *not* allowed to vote, fewer representatives could be sent to Congress.

Douglass and other Negro and white leaders could not accept this proposal. As Douglass pointed out, no part of the Constitution said that people should be kept from voting because of their color or race. If this amendment was accepted, states could keep any group from voting—not only Negroes, but any other group they didn't like.

So it seemed that Douglass and those who agreed with him had more work ahead of them. They had to find a way of convincing Congress that all American adult males should be allowed to vote.

The giant step toward the franchise was made in September 1866. At that time the National Loyalists' Convention met in Philadelphia. Delegates came from the South, North, East, and West. The purpose of the Convention was to learn about conditions in the South. Then ways would be suggested of making life better there for all people. One of the Conven-

Frederick Douglass attends a party given by the daughter of his former master.

tion's proposals was to give the Negro the right to vote.

Frederick Douglass was one of the delegates from New York State. He was the only Negro going to the Convention. On the train to Philadelphia, many white delegates begged him not to appear. Delegates were to march two-by-two to the Convention hall. The whites feared that the sight of a Negro marching with whites would make the people of Philadelphia angry.

"Nonsense," said Douglass. "The people of my state have sent me, and I will march."

He did, and he met not boos, but cheers. One of the people cheering him was Amanda Sears. She was the daughter of Lucretia Auld, wife of Douglass' former master. Mrs. Auld had been especially kind to Frederick. He remembered her, and he remembered Amanda, too, although she had been only a little girl the last time he had seen her. Now she had come all the way from Maryland to Philadelphia (quite a trip in those days!) to see Douglass in his glory. Later, Amanda and her husband invited Douglass to a party in their home. Douglass was a famous and intelligent man, and Amanda's white guests considered it a great privilege to meet and speak with him. He thought how much times had changed. Not so many years ago, a slave, and now a man that people looked up to with respect, eager to shake his hand.

Douglass had proved himself. And, as it turned out, all Negroes had. As a result of their work, the 15th Amendment to the Constitution became a reality.

ARTICLE XV

The right of the citizens of the United States to vote shall not be denied or abridged by the United States or by any State on account of race, color, or previous condition of servitude.

Congress shall have power to enforce this article by appropriate legislation.

In 1870, when the 15th Amendment was accepted, Ulysses S. Grant was President, the man who had been the Union General during the Civil War. He called the 15th Amendment "a measure of grander importance than any other one act of the kind from the foundation of our free government to the present day."

Now Negroes could vote and send men of their choice to Congress who would help the Negro cause.

CHAPTER 14

More Days of Glory

The Negro was a loyal voter. He treasured the franchise because he had worked so hard to get it. On voting days the Negro would get up very early in the morning so as not to be late in casting his vote.

Because of the 15th Amendment and the Reconstruction Act, Negroes were at last able to elect the people who would represent them in government. For the first time in history, Negroes were elected to the United States Congress. During the Reconstruction, two Negro Senators and fourteen Negro Congressmen served in Washington. They were educated, dedicated men. Some had been self-taught, others had attended colleges and universities. There were many white Congressmen who were no better educated than these Negroes.

Among the Negro Congressmen was Senator Hiram K. Revels of Mississippi. He was a minister, and had been educated at a Quaker school, and later at Knox College in Illinois. When Revels entered the Senate for the first time, he was led to the seat that Jefferson Davis had once had—Davis, the President of the Confederate States. Another Negro Senator, Blanche K. Bruce, served from 1875 to 1881. Bruce was known for his excellent speaking. At one time, he served as temporary chairman of the Republican National Convention. About the same time, Frederick Douglass was named Marshal of the District of Columbia.

These Negro leaders, together with liberal whites, helped pass laws that gave the Negro a real chance to make his way in the world as an equal of the white man. For instance, in 1875 Congress passed a Civil Rights Act which guaranteed that Negroes could use all public accommodations, such as restaurants, railways, and hotels. This Civil Rights Act lasted until 1883. Then it was struck down by the Supreme Court. Later, in 1896, the Supreme Court decided that Negroes should have "separate but equal" public accommodations. It was not until May 17, 1954, that the "separate but equal" clause was said to be unconstitutional.

Government changed within the southern states too, during the Reconstruction. Liberal whites and Negroes came from the North to take a hand in southern politics. Many of these were good men who honestly wanted to set the South back on its feet again as a *free* society. Other newcomers were rascals. They came to the South hoping to make fast money and get power. Nowadays, all these newcom-

After the Civil War, Negroes held many state and federal government positions. Between 1869 and 1901, two Negroes were U. S. Senators and twenty were U. S. Congressmen.

ers, good and bad, are often lumped together and called *carpetbaggers* (a carpetbag was a kind of suitcase). Many poor southern whites worked with these men during the Reconstruction, too. Because they were willing to change, other Southerners called them "scalawags."

Newcomers and poor whites ran the governments in many southern states. Black and Tan governments, they were called. Some bad laws were made, and so were some very good ones. These Black and Tan governments made laws which helped prisons and welfare services to operate better. They established public education in many areas. Even after other groups came to power, many laws made by Black and Tan governments were kept on the books.

In politics, then, the Negro was at last having a voice. Reconstruction also helped him to make a living. After the war was over, many plantation owners drove the Negroes off the farms. But it was not long before white men were asking them to come back. The South has always needed the Negro's labor. Frederick Douglass said that the Negro was "the author of whatever prosperity, beauty, and civilization are now possessed by the South." Before the Civil War, white men had said that only the whip would make the Negro work. Now it was obvious that good pay would make him work even harder. But there was a great difference. With pay, the labor which once made the Negro a slave was now making him free, comfortable, and independent. And the Negro had new power, being free. He could choose not to work, and the farms would go to weeds. Or he could work, and make the farms fruitful. As Douglass said, "the Negro could touch the heart of the South through the pocketbook."

It was not only as a hired laborer that the Negro did well. He did well, too, as a farm-owner. By 1880, in Virginia alone, Negroes owned 80,000 acres of farmland. In Georgia they had almost 400,000 acres of farmland and one-and-a-half million dollars worth of city property.

Negroes also became skilled carpenters, brick-makers, cabinet-makers, and longshoremen. They formed their own labor unions, and in 1869 established the National Negro Labor Congress. Negroes also organized businesses. One, the Chesapeake and Marine Railway and Drydock Company, did well for several years, then folded when hard times came to the nation. Other Negroes became inventors. One, Jan Matzelier, invented a machine which fastened the leather over the soles of shoes and drove in the nails. He sold his patent to the United Shoe Machinery Company, and that company made millions of dollars as a result.

Reconstruction also brought other kinds of opportunities to the Negro. At last he was free to explore his own heart and mind, and do those things which made him happier as a human being. Religion had always meant a great deal. Now the church became the center of his social life. Most Negroes joined independent Negro churches, such as the African Methodist Episcopal, or the AMEZ (Zion), or the National Baptist Convention. Some Negroes stayed with the large white religious groups, but they usually had separate churches. The Negro men also formed lodges and clubs: Masons, Elks, and Knights of Pythias. Through church and lodge, the Negro was able to help his neighbors when they were sick, when there was death in the family, when some family needed food and clothing. No longer did he have to depend on a white "master" to take care of him in such situations.

Negro family life changed. Before the Civil War, a Negro family was always in danger of being separated. At any moment, a slave-owner could break up a family by selling a wife or a husband or a child. Now the family could stay together.

Negro men, who had shown their courage in the war, wanted to go on serving their country. They wanted to be ready in case war should ever come again. So during the Reconstruction, most southern states had Negro militia units. There were three in Georgia, one each in Atlanta, Augusta, and Savannah. The men met regularly to drill. They were led by a Negro lieutenant colonel. Each year the men went into summer training, and on holidays they

Education was very important to the former slaves. They wanted to learn to read and write so they could lead better lives.

paraded. The Negro community was proud of these militia groups.

If there was one thing the Negro had yearned for in his days of slavery, it was education. To Frederick Douglass, education had been the beginning of freedom. Now that freedom was won, Negroes wanted education so that they could use the freedom wisely. There was a great thirst for learning. Schools sprang up all over the South. It was not just children who went to learn, but adults, too. Few were too young, and none too old. Negroes wanted to learn to read and write, to spell, to do arithmetic, to find out, to explore. With the Government's help, Negro colleges were started: Fisk, Atlanta, Howard. School teachers came from far and wide to help in the new schools.

And for the man who had no time to go to school, who had to be always busy earning a living in the field, there was always a book. In slavery days, a Negro would have been punished for reading when he was supposed to be laboring. Now, during Reconstruction, it became a usual sight to see a Negro leaning on a plow for a moment as he studied his blue-back speller.

CHAPTER 15

Shadows Fall

Freedom for the Negro was an idea. Many good men, black and white, fought for the idea. The men died, and part of the idea went with them. Lincoln had gone long before. Thaddeus Stevens and Charles Sumner passed away. Frederick Douglass was getting old. Negroes who remembered the glory and the courage of fighting for freedom—well, they were getting few and far between.

Another idea was moving in to take the place of the idea of freedom. This was the idea of money. In the North, factories were springing up. Millions of people were coming from Europe to work in big cities. The factories were a source of great wealth. As industry and business got bigger, more people devoted their energy to making money. Politicians became involved in pleasing the businessman.

Whites were not the only ones to be infected by the money-bug. Some Negro businessmen felt its bite too. In Washington, D.C., some Negro businessmen had started the Freedmen's Saving and Trust Company. The bank had branches in all the southern states. The Washington office was considered one of the most beautiful in the city. It had black walnut walls and marble counters, and the clerks were dressed in only the very best. Negroes put millions of dollars into the bank—hard-earned money. They felt so pleased to be able to earn this money, and to save it for the future.

Frederick Douglass was a trustee of the bank, and was later made its president. All this time, he thought the bank was an honest business. When he was made president, he said he often thought of the contrast "between Frederick the slave boy, running about with only a tow linen shirt to cover him, and Frederick—president of a bank counting its assets in the millions." But while he was president, Douglass discovered that he was the only trustee who had money deposited there. He searched further, and found that the bank had invested money and lost it. There was $40,000 missing which nobody could account for. Because of this and other losses, the bank could pay back only seventy-two cents for every dollar deposited. In other words, the bank could not give back to people what they had put in.

Douglass was overcome with shame. He went to a Senate committee and told them of the situation, and the bank had to stop its operations. Negroes lost so much money in the Freedmen's Bank that many of them would never trust a bank again as long as they lived.

After Reconstruction, when the troops left the South, Negroes lost the right to vote.

109

There were many other examples of dishonest business, and many examples of business seeking favors from government. Businessmen wanted to run the South. The great cotton farms there could supply the northern factories with cloth and thread. There was money to be made. In the election of 1876, Rutherford B. Hayes said that if he was elected he would take the troops out of the South. In that way, Hayes won the election. The troops left. The South was again in the hands of the big southern landowners.

When the troops were taken out of the South, disorder broke out again. The troops had at least kept people from rioting and had kept the Negro fairly safe from any white enemies he might have. Now that the troops were gone, white men began to terrorize the Negro. The Ku Klux Klan, which began in 1865, increased its violence. There were race riots and lynchings. Negroes who tried to vote might find their homes burned or their families killed or injured. Gradually Negroes were forced to stop voting. They lost the right to choose men who would help them.

So, the southern Negro began to lose the rights he had won during the Civil War and Reconstruction. The law called him a free man. But his head and heart told him that indeed he was not allowed to act like one.

Most southern Negroes remained in the South.

Others left when hard times came. The South was beginning to remind them too much of slavery. Some Negroes went north to look for work. There they met with other kinds of hard feelings. White laborers in the North didn't want competition from Negroes. Negroes were not allowed to join white labor unions, so they formed their own. But here again they met with difficulty. Some Negro union leaders were dishonest, and worked closely with the employer to keep Negro wages lower than the wages of the white workers.

A few years after the Civil War, Negroes again found themselves to be the forgotten men, the half-citizens. What had all that struggle been for? What had that War been about? What was it that Lincoln had said at Richmond just a few days before he died? . . . "if those that claim to be your superiors do not know that you are free, take the sword and bayonet and teach them that you are—for God created all men free."

Today, Negroes have taken up the battle again. They fight not with the sword and bayonet, but with the full force of the Federal law behind them. For this time the fight is not to *win* freedom. It was won a hundred years ago. The fight now is to insure that every person can get the rights of full citizenship promised by the Constitution.

Index

115

Index

Index

Reconstruction, 89–94, 96–99, 101–3, 106
Republican Party, 80, 99
Revels, Hiram K., 98–99
Revolts, Negro, 12–17
Richmond, Virginia, 14, 69

Savannah, Georgia, 103
Scalawags, 101
Schools. *See* Education
Sears, Amanda, 96
Senate, 93–94, 98, 108
"Separate but equal" clause, 99
Shaw, Robert Gould, 42, 43, 45, 48, 52–53
Sherman, William T., 60
Ships, slave, 9
Singing, 69, 72–76
Smalls, Robert, 59
Songs, 69, 72–76
Southampton County, Virginia, 15
South Carolina, 3, 14, 37, 44, 76
Speakers, antislavery, 28–31. *See also* specific speakers
Stevens, Thaddeus, 85–86, 89, 107
Suicides of slaves, 9, 12
Sumner, Charles, 93, 107
Supreme Court, 9, 65, 99

Tennessee, 39, 58, 90
Texas, 37

Thirteenth Amendment, 64–65
Tillman, William, 59
Torture of prisoners, 53–54, 55, 58–59
Tubman, Harriet, 23–25, 59
Turner, Nat, 15

Underground Railroad, 18–25
Union Army, 35, 38–54, 55–60, 61–64; and Confederate surrender, 66; song of, 75; and start of war, 3–6 ff
Union Navy, 59
Unions, labor, 76, 102, 111
United Shoe Machinery Company, 102

Vesey, Denmark, 14–15
Virginia, 14, 15, 16, 17, 102. *See also* specific places
Voting, 90, 91–97

Washington, George, 19
Washington, D.C., 36, 70, 107–8
"We are Building a Strong Union", 76
"We are Climbing Jacob's Ladder", 76
"We shall Overcome", 76
West Virginia, 17, 37